Painted Pieces
in a weekend

Julie Collins

JOURNEY EDITIONS
Boston • Tokyo

Simple to make...

...in a weekend

AUTHOR'S ACKNOWLEDGMENTS

I would like to thank my husband and colleague, Charles Lown, for his assistance on this book, especially for his DIY skills which make all things possible.

First published in the United States in 2000 by Journey Editions, an imprint of Periplus Editions (HK) Ltd, with editorial offices at 153 Milk Street, Boston, Massachusetts 02109.

Copyright © 2000 Merehurst Limited
Originally published by Merehurst Limited in 1998.

ISBN: 1-58290-022-1

Distributed in the U.S. by
TUTTLE PUBLISHING
DISTRIBUTION CENTER
Airport Industrial Park
364 Innovation Drive
North Clarendon, VT 05759-9436
Tel: (800) 526-2778
Tel: (802) 773-8930

Printed in Hong Kong
First U.S. edition
06 05 04 03 02 01 00
10 9 8 7 6 5 4 3 2 1

CONTENTS

INTRODUCTION 4
Antiqued **key box** 6
Classic **tray** 10
Grapes and vines **water set** 13
Children's **chair** 16
Limed **picture frame** 20
Gilded **curtain pole** 23
Verdigris **candlestick** 26
Stamped ceramic **tiles** 30
Eastern treasure **chest** 33
Jewelry **box** 36
Indian temple **cushions** 40
Tin-paneled **cupboard** 43

Marbled **plaster pieces** 46
Chrome-effect **frames** 50
Voile **curtain** 53
Stenciled **animal prints** 56
Sponged **lamp base** 60
Oriental **table** 63
Frosted **glass panel** 66
Topiary **cupboard** 70
Mexican painted **pot** 73
TEMPLATES 76
GLOSSARY 78
SUPPLIERS 79
INDEX 80

INTRODUCTION

I have written this book to inspire people who enjoy being creative to tackle simple exciting projects. Don't worry if you have never tried anything like this before - if you follow the instructions, you can easily create beautiful painted pieces on different mediums such as wood, glass, fabric or ceramics and make quick inexpensive projects.

Small wooden boxes, children's chairs, small drawer units and other accessories are fairly cheap to buy and readily available, or you can paint old pieces you already

have, so there is very little initial outlay and you can decorate your first piece with confidence. All the paints, mediums and accessories that I have used are available in DIY stores or super-stores and there are also many mail order companies supplying these items (see the list of addresses on page 79). When you have mastered the techniques used on these projects, I hope that you will have the confidence to go on to decorate larger pieces of furniture and decor.

Before the advent of fast-drying paints and mediums, specialist painters and decorators used oil-based products, adding to them various other products which needed undercoating, and long-term drying periods were essential. If you are familiar with modern paint techniques, you will be aware that up-to-date acrylic mediums dry very rapidly, enabling projects to be finished quickly. Quick-drying water-

based crackle mediums, varnishes, and antiquing patinas and waxes are also available. These are also non-toxic and low in odor. For your reference, a full list and description of the materials, tools and techniques used in this book can be found in the glossary (see page 78).

There is a wonderful selection of ornate handles, trimmings, tassels and various other accessories readily available on the market. These can be used to make a plain inexpensive piece look incredible, and give you the opportunity of being adventurous and creative. For example, you can transform a simple box into an Eastern spice chest by adding ornate handles and feet and then painting the box luxuriously, using the distressing technique, gilding and highlighting. You also have the opportunity to use vibrant colors and metallic finishes to create exciting alternatives.

Once you have produced a professional-looking piece, you can then make wonderful personalized gifts for all occasions, as well as using them to enhance your own home. The projects can all be completed in a weekend, by using the quick-drying acrylic mediums and by following the simple step-by-step instructions. Using these methods, you will have no problem in achieving a really professional result of which you can be proud and delighted.

CHECKLIST

- *key box*
- *fine-grade sandpaper*
- *masking tape*
- *2 small paintbrushes*
- *latex paints: olive green, fjord blue*
- *crackle medium*
- *paper picture*
- *acrylic spray varnish*
- *craft glue*
- *burnt umber artist's acrylic paint*

PREPARATION

Rub the box down with fine-grade sandpaper until all the surfaces are smooth; wipe with a dry cloth to remove all dust. Apply masking tape to the inside back panel of the box.

Antiqued key box

A s well as being used to store keys, these boxes can have a variety of useful purposes such as storing children's jewelery and hair accessories. The hooks can easily be moved around to create space as needed. Each one can be decorated in a different style and using different colors, ranging from the subtle, classic colors of sienna and clay to vibrant green, cerise and purple. Alternatively, you can paint them to match your decor, and age them using crackle medium. For the panel, you can use birthday cards or photographs.

1 *Apply masking tape around the panel on the door where the picture is to be applied. This will prevent paint being accidentally brushed on the panel. Using a small paintbrush, apply one coat of olive green latex paint over the inside of the box. Paint the outside of the box and handle (excluding the panel). Allow to dry thoroughly.*

Using a paintbrush, paint a thin coat of crackle medium *2* over the outside of the box (excluding the panel); do not over-brush, as this will spoil the finished effect. Allow to dry. This process can be speeded up by gently rotating a cool hair dryer, at a distance, over the surface.

3 Dilute some fjord blue latex paint with water until it is the thickness of light cream. Apply the paint over the cupboard in long even strokes, avoiding the door panel. Brush in one direction only, from top to bottom or from side to side. Any small gaps of base coat showing through will enhance the finished crackle effect. Allow to dry.

4 If necessary, enlarge or reduce your picture on a photocopier to the correct size. Spray the picture with a fixing spray or acrylic varnish to seal it. When dry, cut the picture to size, making sure it fits the door panel. Coat the back of the picture with glue and stick it on the panel. Smooth it down carefully with a clean cloth and leave to dry.

More ideas

Once you have mastered the art of crackling paint, you can try different combinations of colors to suit your room decor, choosing colors that show off the effect of the crackle. Use unusual pictures or a family photograph, or make your own stencil to stick in the door panel.

5 Squeeze a small amount of burnt umber artist acrylic paint in a palette or saucer and mix it with a small amount of water. Dip the tip of a brush in the paint and smudge it along the top and side edges of the box, around the handle and lightly around the edges of the picture. Allow to dry. Spray a light coat of varnish over the box and picture. When dry, apply a second coat of varnish to seal. Alternatively, apply a coat of acrylic wax or household furniture wax over the surface for a soft sheen.

A base coat of gold with lilac on top is perfect for carrying a deep purple emperor's head.

Bright yellow and apple green are a refreshing combination for the kitchen, hall or conservatory.

Scandinavian blue and parchment have been used in interiors to great effect for a long time. Here the colors are reversed, with the blue as a base coat and the cream as the top coat.

TIPS

A matte (flat) finish water-based paint is ideal for crackling. Some satin-finish paints have a waxy quality and do not crackle so well. If the paint should start streaking or running, leave it alone. When it is dry, rub the surface down gently with fine-grade sandpaper, apply a coat of dead flat acrylic varnish and then proceed as in the steps. Ageing is optional—you might prefer to leave your box with just the paint effect.

- *tray*
- *fine-grade sandpaper*
- *primer spray paint*
- *face mask*
- *white acrylic spray paint, enamel paint or decorative pearlized paint*
- *photocopied motifs*
- *scissors*
- *small artist's brush*
- *glue*
- *fine-nibbed black permanent pen*
- *small paint roller*
- *acrylic varnish*

PREPARATION

Wash the tray thoroughly to remove any dirt or grease. Then, when dry, rub the tray down with fine-grade sandpaper. This roughens the surface, creating a "key" for the paint to adhere to.

Classic tray

An old tray can quickly be transformed into a timeless classic with some spray paint and black and white photocopies. Look through books and magazines to find suitable pictures of old statues and urns; these can then be reduced or enlarged on a photocopier and duplicated as necessary to decorate your tray. I also photocopied some text to put underneath. If you like, you could type blocks of ornate script on a computer and then cut out the print-outs to use for decoration. Finally, to protect the decorated surface and make the tray durable, simply apply a coat of varnish.

1 *Shake the can of primer spray paint vigorously before use. Mask all surrounding areas, then, wearing a face mask, spray an even coat of primer all over the tray. Use an even, sweeping motion from side to side, taking care not to apply too thick a coat which could create runs in the paint. Allow to dry thoroughly. To speed up drying time, you can use a hair dryer on low heat, holding it a short distance away from the surface and rotating it gently so as not to overheat the paint.*

Piranesi's "Vasi" Gryphons 1778

erotomachis 1497

2 Apply an even coat of white acrylic spray paint over the surface of the tray. Leave to dry for 20 to 40 minutes; drying times will vary according to the temperature of the surroundings. To achieve a denser covering, apply a second coat when dry. You can speed up the drying process using a hair dryer as in Step 1.

3 Spray the sheet of photocopied motifs with spray varnish to prevent the ink from the photocopies bleeding. Allow to dry. Then carefully cut around the edges of the motifs with sharp scissors. Motifs in an assortment of different sizes can look very effective. Cut out pieces of descriptive text to mount underneath the pictures.

4 Arrange the motifs on the tray. Then place them face down on a piece of paper. Brush glue on to the back of each motif. Then reposition the glued motifs on the tray and wipe them with a soft dry cloth, to ensure that the edges are well glued and that there are no trapped air bubbles. Using a permanent black pen with a fine nib, draw around the edge of each picture and block of text.

5 Allow the glue to dry, then, using a small paint roller, apply two coats of acrylic varnish over the top of the glued motifs, allowing the first coat to dry before applying the second. Allow the varnish to dry thoroughly and harden before use.

Grapes and vines water set

Glass painting has become extremely popular recently as it offers an instant way to transform perfume bottles, decanters, glasses and window panels. This set of glasses and a jug has been painted in rich glowing green and purple to create a picture of grapes and vines, but you can paint other motifs using any combination of marble, lustre, metallic and glitter glass paint. A word of warning though, do not put your masterpieces in the dishwasher or the paint will float away! Instead, wash hand-painted glass with warm soapy water.

CHECKLIST

- *glass jug*
- *glasses*
- *paint thinner*
- *silver and grey contour outlining medium*
- *cotton swabs*
- *fine artist's brush*
- *glass paint: purple, leaf green*

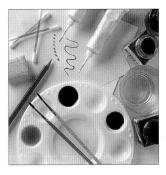

PREPARATION

Wash the glassware in warm soapy water and allow to dry, then wipe it down with a soft cotton cloth and paint thinner to remove any labels, glue, grease or dirt. Allow to dry.

1 *Draw a bunch of grapes on a piece of paper, if possible copying from a real bunch for greater accuracy. Draw half-grapes at the outer edges of the bunch and full ones in the front; the bunch should be wider at the top and taper to a small single grape angled at the bottom.*

2 Gently squeezing a tube of contour outlining medium, paint the outline of the design on to the glass jug. You will need to create a three-piece stalk with leaves on either side, with additional inner lines for veins and a bunch of grapes hanging underneath. You might find it more reassuring to practice using the contour outlining medium on a piece of glass first. Remove any smudges with a cotton swab dipped in paint thinner, then leave to dry.

3 Dip the artist's brush into green glass paint, taking care not to overload the brush, and then paint inside the outline of the leaves and stalk with flowing strokes. The outlines will prevent the paint from seeping through to other parts of the design. The paint will start to dry quickly so work rapidly and deftly to produce a clear and even finish. Paint inside the grapes with the purple paint in the same way. Allow to dry.

4 Paint a spiral of winding grape vines around the glasses with leaves going in different directions. When dry, add the veining on the leaves with contour outlining medium. Then stand the glasses and the jug upside down and paint the bottoms green.

TIPS

When painting decanters and glasses, place them on a plate so that you can slowly rotate this to work around the surfaces easily. Hold stem glasses by their bases and work from the top downwards; you can then stand the glass base down on a flat surface to complete it without leaving any finger marks. Use the gold or silver outlining medium for a more luxurious finish. Stained glass window effects can be achieved by using the grey outlining medium.

- *child's chair*
- *medium-grade sandpaper*
- *face mask*
- *acrylic primer spray paint*
- *decorative spray paint:*
yellow, sky blue
- *stencil*
- *spray mount*
- *template plastic*
- *permanent pen*
- *cutting board*
- *craft knife*
- *stencil brushes sizes 2 & 3*
- *acrylic stencil paint:*
leaf green, heather, blue
- *acrylic spray varnish*

PREPARATION

Clean the chair thoroughly to remove any dirt or wax, and sand down the surface to a fine finish. Carefully check that there are no screw or nail heads protruding; if there are, either hammer them into the wood, or prise them out.

Children's chair

Children love to have personalized chairs decorated with their favorite characters, designs and names. Chairs also make wonderful gifts, as they often stay in the family, and are passed down from one generation to another. Old chairs can be found very cheaply when schools are refurbished; alternatively, you can revamp a child's chair you already have. I have created a specialized chair for my niece and nephew and I know they will be thrilled with it.

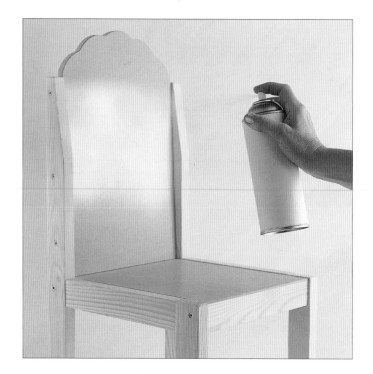

1 *Turn the chair upside down and, wearing a face mask, spray the underneath and the legs of the chair with the plain base coat, then turn the chair over and spray the rest of it, taking care not to apply too heavy a coat as this could cause runs in the paint. Allow to dry thoroughly. Using a cool hair dryer will speed up the drying time.*

Shake the can of yellow spray paint. Then, holding it approximately 10in (25cm) away from the chair, spray **2** a thin coat of paint evenly in a sweeping motion over the underneath, legs, seat and part way up the back of the chair. Place a piece of card or paper on the seat, then spray the sky blue paint from the end of the yellow to the top of the chair and down the back. Allow to dry. Apply a second coat, commencing with the blue; when you use the yellow spray, bring the can further back and apply a very fine mist over the bottom half of the blue paint, becoming denser on reaching the seat, to blend the sand and sky together. Allow to dry.

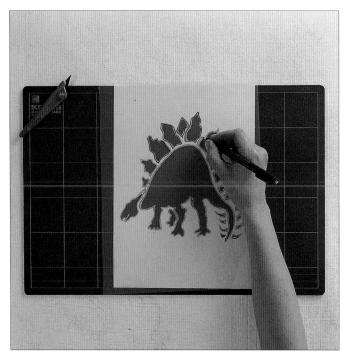

3 Enlarge the stencil design on page 76, if desired. Apply spray mount to a sheet of plastic and place this on top of the template to prevent it slipping. Trace the design with a permanent pen. Place the template plastic on a cutting board. Cut out the design with the craft knife. Repeat to make further stencils if desired.

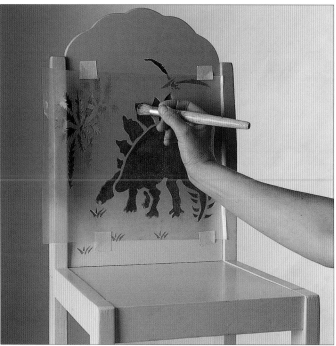

4 Spray the back of each stencil with spray mount, and position it on the back and seat of the chair. Dip the tip of a stencil brush into acrylic stencil paint, wipe off any excess and, using stabbing strokes, apply paint through the cut stencil. Mix blue and yellow paint to make the green for the trees and red and blue for the purple dinosaur.

5 Allow the paint to dry. Then spray an even coat of varnish over the painted chair for protection, and leave to dry. Further coats of varnish can be applied if required. Follow the spraying methods described in Step 2.

More ideas
If your child does not like dinosaurs or you would prefer a more feminine design for the chair, use different colors and stencils. If you do not feel you are ready to attempt stencilling or stamping, you can still achieve an unusual look by spraying the two-color effect shown here in ultraviolet orange and yellow.

This chair for a little angel has been sprayed in English rose and stamped with yellow and pale blue daisies.

A zingy ultraviolet chair in bright orange and yellow will glow in the dark with torches or nightlights.

The jungle theme is sprayed on this chair in sand yellow and stencilled with terracotta for tiger stripes.

Limed picture frame

PREPARATION

Clean the frame thoroughly with wire wool dipped in distilled turpentine to remove any build-up of varnish. Then rub it down with a clean cloth and allow to dry.

Limed wood has a timeless look, and is especially effective for enhancing carved pieces. Liming is simple to do and makes a very unusual and attractive frame for a picture. Other grained wood furniture can also be treated in this way to make a fairly plain piece become full of character. You can buy liming kits in different colors which include everything you need (see page 79 for sources), but you must make sure that the wood is well grained so that the liming wax can penetrate it and create the desired bleached effect.

1 *Open up the grain of the wood by brushing firmly along the line of the grain with the wire brush. Some woods are quite soft so do this with care. Then brush over the frame with an old toothbrush to remove all the surplus dust, and wipe with a soft cloth.*

2 *Wearing rubber gloves, take a small pad of wire wool and dip it into liming wax. Then rub the wax generously over the entire frame, especially into all grooves and crevices. This will enable the liming wax to penetrate the wood. Leave for approximately 20 minutes.*

3 *Using plenty of effort and a strong pressing motion across the grain, rub off the excess wax with a soft cotton cloth. This will leave the liming wax in the open grain and patterns of the wood. Buff to a soft sheen.*

4 *Rub a soft cotton cloth lightly into neutral furniture wax and gently polish the surface of the wood. The idea is to create a finished surface without disturbing the limed effect in the grain.*

T I P

Neutral wax has a grey tone and is ideal for use on limed wood, whereas clear and yellow waxes have a creamy yellow coloring which would spoil the effect.

Gilded curtain pole

Ornate curtain poles are very expensive to buy, but you can create your own quite easily by using an existing pole or by buying an inexpensive plain curtain pole. You can also buy or have made a wrought iron pole with finials and rings which is very fashionable as it is, but can also be effectively transformed into Victorian splendor with dark red paint and gold leaf. Gilding is now easy to do using gold or metal transfer leaf.

CHECKLIST

- *curtain pole finials and rings*
- *distilled turpentine*
- *medium-grade sandpaper*
- *red oxide paint or deep red traditional paint*
- *paintbrush*
- *acrylic gold size*
- *gold or metal transfer leaf*
- *soft-bristled flat brush*
- *lint-free cotton cloth*
- *gloss varnish*

PREPARATION

Clean the metal pole thoroughly with a soft cloth dipped in distilled turpentine to remove any oil or grease. When dry, rub down with sandpaper. Wipe with a clean cloth to remove any dust.

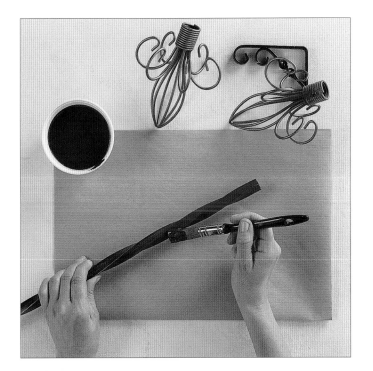

1 *Apply a coat of dark red paint over the pole, finials, rings and attachments. You can use red oxide spray paint as an alternative, but do not use oil-based paint as this will inhibit the action of the acrylic size. Allow to dry.*

2 Brush acrylic gold size liberally over the entire pole, finials and rings. Lay the pole between two stands to enable you to twist it to allow access. Leave for at least 15 minutes for the size to become tacky, when it will be ready to receive the gold leaf.

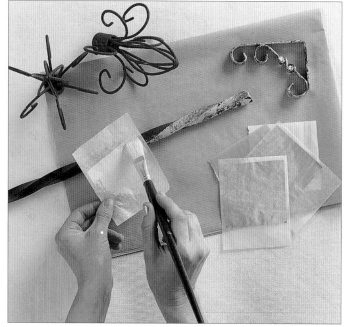

3 Place one piece of transfer gold leaf, gold side down, on the pole. Using a firm-bristled brush, gently press a small section of the leaf on to the pole; the leaf will transfer itself to the pole with light pressure. Place the leaf in random patterns over the pole, leaving irregular sections of the pole without any leaf, thus exposing the base coat. This will create an antiqued look. Repeat this process on the finials and rings.

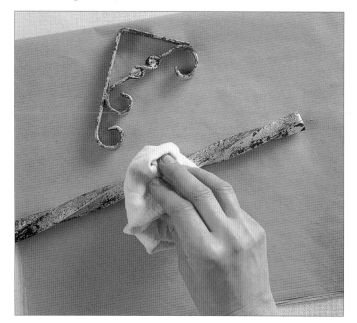

4 Brush away any loose pieces of gold leaf with the brush. Leave to dry, then gently buff the gilded surface with a clean lint-free cotton cloth to achieve a high sheen. Protect with a coat of varnish.

TIPS

An easy way to make a fabric curtain is to cut out a piece of fabric one and a half times the width of your window and the required length, allowing for hems. Line or roll edge the side seams. Press the curtain and measure equal spacing along the top edge of the curtain for the appropriate number of rings. Then simply clip the rings on to the marked place on the fabric and hang the curtain.

Verdigris candlestick

CHECKLIST

- *candlestick*
- *fine-grade sandpaper*
- *verdigris kit or latex paint: sludge brown, pale green, dark green*
- *paintbrush*
- *2 stencil brushes*
- *gilt wax or gold stencil stick*
- *satin spray varnish*

PREPARATION

Using fine-grade sandpaper, gently sand all the surfaces of the candlestick, then wipe off the resulting dust with a soft cotton cloth.

Candlesticks are ideal accessories to revamp in a range of different styles. This project shows how you can transform an old brass candlestick simply and cheaply with an effect of antique copper verdigris. For this dramatic and elegant look, you will need a verdigris kit, or you can simply use latex paints and gilt wax. To create a very grand candlestick as a festive table centerpiece, you can hang crystal and glass beads in swags and droplets from the arms.

1 *Paint the entire candlestick with brown latex paint, applying a generous coat to cover all the surfaces completely. Allow to dry thoroughly.*

Pour some light green paint into the lid of the container and dip the stencil brush into the paint, coating the tip well. Wipe off any excess on a cloth. Using a firm stippling motion, dab paint over the candlestick to create a mottled or speckled effect, allowing some of the base coat to show through. Allow to dry.

2

3 Pour some dark green paint into the lid of the container and dip in a dry stencil brush, wiping off excess paint on a cloth. With light feathery strokes, highlight the raised parts of the candlestick, the patterns on the arms, and around the candle bases. This color will contrast with the main coat of pale green paint, which will be visible in some places.

4 Wearing rubber gloves, rub your thumb or finger over a gilt wax or stencil stick. Gently rub small amounts of the gold coloring on to the edges, rims, raised parts and patterns of the candlestick to create a burnished effect.

5 Spray a light coat of satin varnish over the entire candle-stick to preserve the finish. Allow to dry thoroughly.

More ideas
Recreating the effect of verdigris on objects in the home and garden can be used to enhance and revamp old pieces or to create stylish accessories at minimal cost. You may have a high tech home, in which case you can choose different styles and effects on objects such as lights, wall sconces and vases.

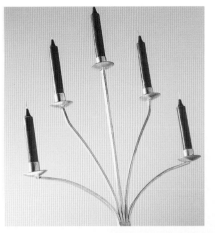

This candlestick was sludge green, but has come to life with this special chrome paint effect.

Bronzing can be achieved by the same process as verdigris, using dark brown, light brown and bronze-gold.

Be bold and adventurous and add bright colored candles instead of white or cream.

- *ceramic tiles*
- *abrasive pad*
- *enamel spray paint: Dutch blue or bright green*
- *face mask*
- *ceramic paint: white or terracotta and yellow*
- *saucer or paint palette*
- *4in (10cm) tile stamp*
- *stamp roller or short-haired paintbrush*

PREPARATION

Remove any dirt or grease from the tiles using distilled turpentine and a clean cloth. Allow to dry. Rub the tiles thoroughly with an abrasive pad to create a "key" for the paint to adhere to. Wipe the surface again with a clean cloth to remove any dust.

Stamped ceramic tiles

Stamping is a quick and easy way to customize your tiles, adding color and style to plain white tiles at a fraction of the cost of re-tiling. Stamping is similar to stencilling, although it does not have the same definition, but it is very simple and can be used to great effect. Try stamping individual tiles to make coasters or plant stands, or transform a set of tiles for a tray, tabletop or backsplash. Ceramic paints are available in a wide range of colors. The Dutch blues and whites used here will suit a country or classic look, and would be ideal for a backsplash on a wash stand.

1 *Wearing a face mask, apply the blue enamel spray paint in light even coats as this will give a smoother finish. Leave to dry. To speed up the drying time, use a cool hair dryer, holding it a minimum of 7in (17.5cm) away from the tiles.*

2 Pour a small amount of white ceramic paint into a saucer or palette. Dip the round flat top of the roller into the paint, then gently apply this to the stamp by pressing the flat face of the roller against the raised patterned areas of the stamp. Alternatively, use a short-haired paintbrush, dipping it in the paint first and then applying it to the stamp with a stabbing motion.

3 Leave the stamp for a few moments until the paint becomes tacky and then press the stamp hard on to the center of the tile, first pressing in the center of the stamp, then rocking back and forth to ensure that the entire pattern is transferred to the tile. You might find it worthwhile to practice stamping on a piece of paper before stamping on the tile so you can perfect your technique.

4 You could apply complementary paint colors like terra-cotta and yellow on a bright green base. Pick out areas of the pattern for the first color, clean the roller, then apply the second color to the remaining raised patterns. Stamp the tile as above.

TIPS

Do not overload the stamp with paint, especially in between the raised areas of the pattern, as this will result in smudges. If you do get any excess paint or smudges, however, these can be cleaned off quickly using distilled turpentine and a clean cloth. Some ceramic paints need to be baked; read instructions carefully. Ceramics that have been painted with ceramic paint should be hand-washed and not put into a dishwasher.

Eastern treasure chest

There are many small units and chests available in large DIY superstores that are ready to paint at a very low cost. These can easily be transformed into wonderfully original and unusual chests for use as spice containers and treasure chests, or storage drawers for bathroom soaps, lotions and cosmetics. All you need to use are latex paints resembling the true pigment colors of clay, sienna, lime and old white. Then, if you add ring handles and ornate feet you can create an aged mystic Eastern chest which would be perfect for the kitchen, bathroom, bedroom or study of your home.

CHECKLIST

- *chest*
- *drill*
- *sandpaper*
- *paintbrushes*
- *latex paint: mid-brown, old white*
- *moist towelettes*
- *brass ring handles*
- *4 ornate feet*
- *neutral furniture wax*

PREPARATION

Drill holes in the back of the drawers for the handles, and at the base of the chest for feet to be fitted. Rub down the entire cabinet with sandpaper, then wipe off excess dust with a damp cloth.

1 *Using the paintbrush, apply mid-brown paint over the inside and outside of the drawers and the entire chest, including the feet. Allow to dry. Gently sand off any paint build-up or runs with the moist towelettes. Wipe off any excess dust with a soft cotton cloth.*

2 Dip a dry paintbrush into the old white paint, wiping off
  excess on to a dry cloth. Paint this lightly over the chest,
using long strokes in one direction, top to bottom or side to
side, to create a streaky effect; leave the corners and slight
edges uncovered in places. Allow to dry. Gently rub the chest
down with moist towelettes, using more pressure on some of
the corners. Remove excess dust with a soft cloth.

3 Attach the handles to the drawers and secure them
  firmly on the inside with the nuts provided; if the center
screw is too long, cut it using side snips. Screw ornate feet to
the bottom four corners of the chest, fastening them from the
inside of the chest.

4 Squeeze a small amount of burnt umber artist's acrylic
  paint into a container and add a little water and mix.
Dip your finger into the paint and gently smudge it over the
edges and grooves of the chest, around the handles and
finger holes. Allow to dry thoroughly. Gently distress by
rubbing back with fine wet-and-dry paper.

5 Using a soft cotton cloth and neutral furniture wax,
  apply a generous coating of wax all over the chest. Allow
to stand for 20 minutes, then gently buff to a soft sheen. If
desired, you can add further coats of polish which will add
greater protection and create a deeper sheen.

Jewelry box

You do not have to study the ancient art of calligraphy to achieve these stunning results. Instead, you can create names and sentences simply by using the template letters featured on page 76. Using decorative script adds a stylish and original touch to a jewelry box. For further inspiration, try visiting your local library and looking at books on calligraphy and Latin writings. Calligraphy pens and brushes made from bamboo with specially shaped tips are readily available from art shops. Gold and silver flow calligraphy pens are also suitable for this purpose and are extremely easy to use.

PREPARATION

Rub the box down with fine-grade sandpaper, then wipe off the surplus dust with a clean cloth. Remove all catches and hinges. Remove or mask off the mirror carefully.

1 *Place a jar of gesso in a bowl with hot water and leave it until it becomes hot and runny, then paint it over the box while it is of this consistency. Allow to dry, then rub gently with fine-grade sandpaper. Repeat the process two or three more times to obtain a glass-smooth surface.*

2 Carefully paint around the mirror frame and inside of the box with parchment flat acrylic paint and leave to dry. Using a paintbrush or small paint roller, cover the rest of the box with two coats of the same paint, allowing to dry between each coat. Using fine-grade sandpaper, gently rub down the painted surface, paying particular attention to any build-up of paint on corners and edges. Wipe off any excess dust with a dry cloth.

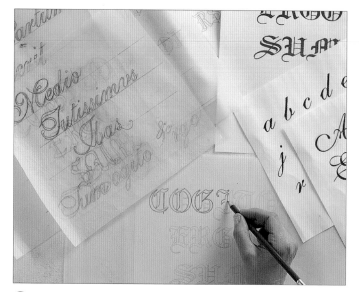

3 Using the tracing paper and pencil, trace over the calligraphy letters in the template section (see page 76) and make a name, sentences, or poem, or simply create patterns using the scrolls. The calligraphy can either be created in lines, blocks or at random. You will need to trace enough calligraphy to cover the lid and sides of the jewelry box and around the mirror frame; alternatively, you could just decorate the lid if preferred.

4 Lay the transfer paper on to the box, place the tracing paper on top of this and draw over the outlines of all the letters, words and scrolls again, pressing gently with the pencil. When you remove the paper, there will be a faint col-ored outline on the box to follow for your painting.

5 Dip a calligraphy brush into brown ink and gently paint along the transferred lines, making part of the letters thin and other parts thicker. Leave to dry. Using the same technique, paint individual letters around the mirror frame. Leave the box open to dry.

6 Brush a thin, even coat of acrylic varnish over the box and allow to dry. Treat the inside of the box in the same way and allow to dry. Then apply a second coat of varnish. When dry, replace all hinges and catches on the box.

More ideas
You can be as subtle or as adventurous as you like when decorating a jewelry box. Classic dark colors and rich gold give the effect of Victorian splendor and luxury while black and cream have great monochromatic impact; alternatively you can simply use any combination of colors that match your decor.

This box has been decorated with parchment emulsion and brown ink to recreate old parchment styles.

Another classic option is deep Victorian red and bold lettering in glorious gold.

Black and cream are very strong together. Mix and match different styles of calligraphy.

- silk cushions
- cardboard
- blotting paper
- stencil
- spray mount
- acrylic metallic and pearlized fabric paint
- palette or saucer
- stencil brushes, sizes 1 and 2
- template plastic

PREPARATION

Remove the cushion covers and wash them. Press the fabric, ensuring there are no creases. Select a pattern from the templates on page 76 and make a stencil following the instructions on page 18. Cut cardboard and blotting paper to fit inside the cushion cover; these will absorb any excess paint that seeps through the fabric.

Indian temple cushions

These silk cushions in vibrant Far Eastern colors are decorated with metallic paint, then edged with ornate tassels for a touch of luxury. Other soft furnishings such as lampshades and curtains can also be hand-painted or stencilled, enabling numerous styles to be created, ranging from fleurs-de-lis for a traditional effect to exotic silk flowers for glamor. You can make your own tassels by using natural fabrics such as jute, silk, gold thread and cording.

1 *When combining colors, it is advisable to practice stencilling on paper before starting your cushion covers. Lightly spray the back of the stencil with spray mount, place it on the paper and smooth down carefully. Dip the stencil brush in the paint, dab off the excess on a cloth, then "rub" the paint through the stencil using a circular motion. The secret is not to have too much paint on the brush. Remove the stencil to see the effect.*

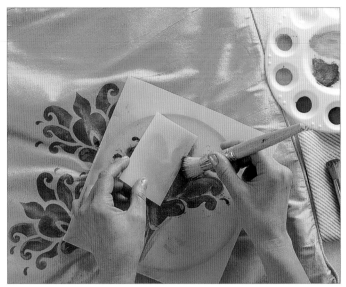

2 Choose the color you wish to use on the cushion cover and squeeze a small amount of paint on to a palette. Dip the end of the stencil brush in the paint, wiping off any excess on to a damp cloth. Using a circular motion, apply the metallic fabric paint through the stencil. Remove the stencil carefully and allow the paint to dry.

3 To work in two different colors, mask off any areas for the second color with template plastic when applying the first color. Then repeat the process to apply the second color, this time masking off the first color. Remove the stencil carefully and allow to dry.

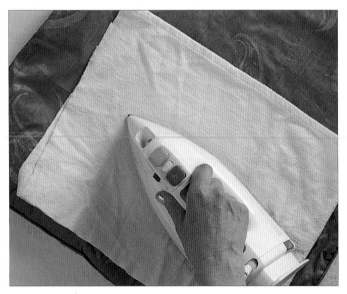

4 Some fabric paints need heat sealing, so read the manufacturer's instructions carefully. When the paint is dry, remove the cardboard from underneath the fabric, but leave the blotting paper in position. Then place a dry cotton cloth over the cushion cover and iron over the cloth with a hot iron to heat-seal the paint. When cool, remove the blotting paper and gently put the cover on the cushion.

MAKING TASSELS

You can make your own tassels by cutting several 6in (15cm) lengths of different colored embroidery floss. Keeping the lengths together, fold them in half and tie a length of thread around the folded threads close to the looped end; cut off the thread ends to neaten. Shake and trim the ends of the tassel. Add tassels to the corners and zip fasteners of the cushions for extra decoration.

Tin-panelled cupboard

A pplying metal decorative panels is a way of customizing a box, small cupboard or door panel. You can buy small pieces of sheet metal from the plumbing section of a hardware store or other DIY stores; have it cut to size or cut it yourself with tin snips or specialized scissors. I decorated the panel of a kitchen cupboard door with a star, but you can of course create your own design using any motif.

CHECKLIST

- *cupboard or doors*
- *sandpaper*
- *paintbrush*
- *latex paint*
- *sheet metal*
- *spray mount*
- *tin snips or specialized scissors*
- *marker pen*
- *tracing paper*
- *cardboard*
- *center punch*
- *small hammer*
- *epoxy resin glue or fine panel pins*

PREPARATION

Remove the door from the cupboard. Rub both down with sandpaper. Paint the cupboard and the outside of the door in the color of your choice, then allow to dry.

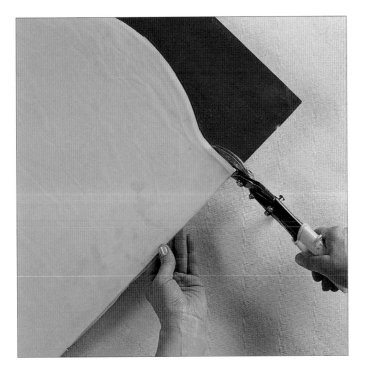

1 *Place the sheet metal on to a firm surface. Cut a paper pattern the exact size of your door panel and, using spray mount, position it on the sheet metal. Draw around the paper pattern with a marker pen. Using tin snips or specialized scissors, carefully cut out the shape.*

2 Using the original paper template, cut a piece of tracing paper to this size. Spray-mount the back of the tracing paper and, using a pencil and ruler, trace the star pattern in the center (see page 76). Peel the tracing paper off. Using a marker pen, mark out dots along all the pattern lines of the star approximately 1/4 in (6mm) apart. Then draw a line around the outside edge of the tracing paper and mark off equally spaced dots along this line.

3 Place the metal panel on a piece of cardboard and spray-mount the paper pattern on top of this; this will stop the pattern moving. Place the point of the center punch on each marked dot at a time and gently tap with the hammer. This will make small indentations in the metal; take care not to hammer too hard or you will perforate the metal surface. Repeat the process to create indentations along all the lines of the star pattern and around the edges.

4 Smear epoxy resin glue over the back of the metal panel and smooth the metal into place on the cupboard door. Allow it to adhere firmly. Alternatively, you can attach the metal using fine panel pins in the corners and edges.

T I P S

If you have used a water-based paint to coat your cupboard, it is advisable to seal this with a coat of clear acrylic varnish. You can also add a metal door knob to match the panel if you wish, or paint the existing wooden one with metallic paint.

Marbled plaster pieces

CHECKLIST

- *plaster piece*
- *fine-grade sandpaper*
- *white satin latex paint*
- *paint tray*
- *mini roller with foam sleeve*
- *acrylic transparent glaze*
- *artist acrylic paints: black, mother-of-pearl, white*
- *hog's hair paintbrush*
- *softening brush*
- *nylon decorator's brush*
- *round artist's brush, no.3*
- *acrylic gloss varnish*

PREPARATION

Rub down the plaster piece with fine sandpaper to remove any lumps and smooth out chips. Then wash the piece with warm soapy water.

Few mediums can compete against the timeless beauty and texture of marble, which is so smooth, durable and attractive when used for floors and sculptures. Although marble is very expensive there are paint techniques you can use to recreate the look of marble. Plaster pieces are smooth in texture and adapt themselves well to faux marbling techniques. Columns, plaques and masks can actually be made to look like pieces that have broken off carved marble.

1 *Pour some white latex paint into a paint tray and use a paint roller to apply an even coat of paint over the plaster piece. Allow to dry, then sand off any raised areas until the surface is smooth, and wipe with a soft cloth to remove any dust. Apply another coat of paint and leave to dry.*

2 Mix the background glazes. Put a tablespoon of acrylic transparent glaze into each of two containers. Squeeze a few drops of mother-of-pearl acrylic paint into one of the containers, and three drops of black acrylic plus one and a half drops of white acrylic into the other container. Stir the glazes well with the end of a paintbrush.

3 Fully load a hog's hair paintbrush and paint smudgy, irregular diagonal bands of glaze on the plaster piece, alternating the mother-of-pearl and the grey glazes. These bands will form the background marble drifts. When tacky, feather the section with a softening brush. Cover the column in stages by painting and feathering in sections.

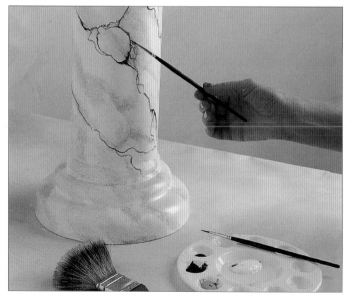

4 When the entire column is covered, leave the glaze to go tacky, then soften it with a softening brush, working in the same direction as the bands of glazes. This will produce a softer, more subtle effect. If the background starts to disappear, leave the glaze to dry for a little longer. After softening, leave the glaze to dry completely.

5 Apply a coat of clear glaze; feather out all brushstrokes. Mix small equal amounts of black artist acrylic and transparent glaze. Fully load a round artist's brush, and working in the same direction as the drifts, pull the brush down diagonally through the glaze, imitating the shape of a tree branch. Soften the veins with the softening brush.

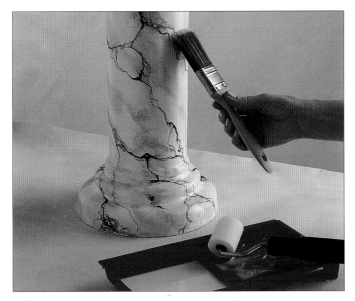

6 When completely dry, apply a coat of acrylic gloss varnish using a nylon decorator's brush, then feather out all brushstrokes. Leave to dry and repeat for maximum protection. Alternatively, apply a coat of acrylic lacquer; this can subsequently be polished using a good-quality car polish. Both varnish and lacquer are heat and water resistant.

More ideas

If you prefer to begin with a smaller piece, there is a variety of plaster pieces available: Greek wall plaques which actually look like broken pieces of old buildings, cherubs, plant shelves, masks, and large columns. When you are more accomplished you could try a stunning marble fireplace, or even a bathroom floor.

A marbled mask makes a stylish alternative to a picture. Carrara marble has a sandy background with pale grey veins.

This unusual and dramatic Potoro marble has a black background with ochre and sienna veining.

Have fun with faux marble; this wall plaque with dancing ladies has a lilac background with bright pink veins running through it.

TIPS

Faux marbling looks most impressive on smooth surfaces, as these imitate best the polished surface of marble. If a softening brush is too expensive, dry off the nylon decorator's brush and use this for all softening stages.

Chrome-effect frames

Simple wooden frames can be transformed into high-tech chrome simply by using paint. This chrome-effect paint is applied with a brush and dries without leaving any brushstrokes; bronze, pewter and metallic blue are all compatible with chrome. Small picture frames are ideal for family photographs or postcards, or look for unusual copyright-free pictures like the ones shown. Paint each frame slightly differently to make an eye-catching set.

1 *Using fine-grade sandpaper, gently rub down the wooden frame, working along the grain until the surface feels smooth. As chrome is normally very smooth, any rough or raised areas would spoil the finished appearance.*

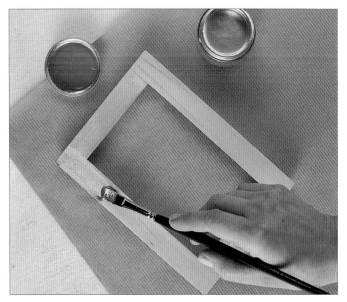

2 Lay the frame on paper. Shake the enamel paint well, then fully load a flat artist's brush with paint. Keeping the flat edge of the brush against the surface, paint the frame using long sweeping strokes in one direction. When you have finished painting, clean the brush immediately with distilled turpentine

3 Check the drying time of your particular paint before painting the corners of the frames with pewter or bronze enamel paint. Use the join of the frame as a starting point and paint a neat square in each corner with two or three strokes including the outside edges as well. Repeat if necessary.

4 When the paint is touch dry, you can decorate the frame further. Dip the artist's liner brush into black acrylic paint, then paint small dots marking the halfway position on each edge of the bronze squares. Then paint a series of dots to make a line between each of the four dots as shown. Allow the paint to dry.

5 To create the appearance of mosaic, paint the corner squares with metallic blue enamel paint as before, using a flat artist's brush. Then, using a pencil, mark out a square an even distance from the edge of each corner square. Paint each of these pencilled squares in metallic blue paint. Leave to dry.

Voile curtain

Decorating a plain piece of voile for any room in the house is an exciting and creative project. Indian sari fabrics look fabulous and are highly decorated with gold, vibrant colors and elaborate designs. In this project, you can create your own designs on plain, but vividly colored voile, using gold and silver outline mediums, glitter glue and sequins. Hand wash the decorated voile carefully in cold water and do not iron as this could ruin the decoration.

PREPARATION

Clear a large covered table so you can move the voile along as you work and keep it flat.

1 *Find some Indian designs and practice drawing them on paper. This project features a climbing tree with leaves, flowers and birds, and simple oval shapes to decorate the edges. Work out the main elements of the design. When you feel confident, you can transfer the design on to the fabric; leave a 4in (10cm) edge unpainted for the hem.*

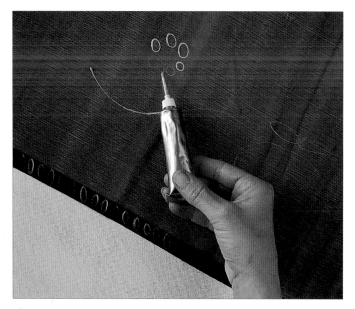

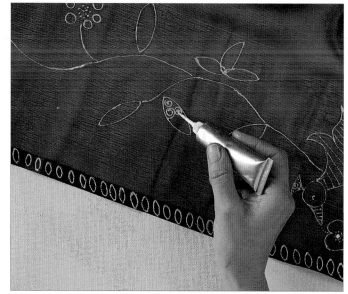

2 *Lay the fabric down flat on paper. Using a fine artist's brush paint the first section of the pattern faintly with gold paint. Point the nozzle of the gold outline medium at the fabric, and pull the voile taut with your other hand. Gently squeeze the tube while following the painted outlines, taking care not to smudge them.*

3 *Using the gold outline medium, fill the bird in with diagonal stripes across its body and wings. Decorate the leaves with gold and silver spirals; to do this, place the tube nozzle on the fabric and work outwards in a circular motion. Fill the centers of the flowers with several small dots. Leave to dry.*

4 *Add color to the design using glitter glue. Decorate the flower petals by squeezing glue in each circle. Using tweezers, push a diamante into the wet glue. Decorate the bird's eye in the same way. Leave to dry before moving on to the next section.*

5 *Allow the outline medium and glue to dry, then turn under the raw edges of the voile by 4in (10cm) to create a hem; sew it neatly by hand and press. For a true Indian flavor, stitch small gold metal bells at intervals along the border pattern using gold thread.*

Stenciled animal prints

CHECKLIST

- *fabric*
- *paper*
- *spray mount*
- *stenciling acetate*
- *permanent pen*
- *cutting mat*
- *craft knife*
- *blotting paper*
- *fabric paint: sienna natural, black*
- *palette*
- *2 stencil brushes, size 2*

PREPARATION

Wash your chosen fabric to remove any residues which might react with the paint, then dry and iron the fabric so that it is free from creases.

Animal prints are very popular in today's fashion and interior design houses; you can find leopard, zebra, giraffe, tiger and more on many fabrics. In this project, you can evoke an exciting African or Indian atmosphere. Look around to find the texture and color of material you prefer. Synthetic suede and leather, and even velvet, are all suitable fabrics on to which you can stencil animal prints.

1 *To stencil the leopard print design, enlarge the two templates on page 77 to the required size. Alternatively, copy a print from another source and draw a pattern of the shapes. Spray a thin coat of spray mount on the back of a piece of stenciling acetate and place it over the first leopard design. Trace outlines with a permanent pen. Repeat with a second piece of stenciling acetate to make the second stencil.*

Peel each piece of acetate off the paper, place it on a **2** cutting mat and cut along all the pen outlines with a craft knife. Push out the cut pieces carefully as acetate tears easily which may make the stencil leak.

3 Place the fabric down flat on blotting paper. Secure the first stencil on top with spray mount. Dip the stencil brush into a small amount of sienna natural fabric paint and dab off any excess. Apply through the stencil, working gently in a circular motion. Load the brush as necessary.

4 Peel off the first stencil. Place the second stencil over the painted fabric, aligning the shapes in the print. Using black fabric paint and a clean stencil brush, apply the paint as in Step 3. When you have finished, peel the acetate away carefully to avoid smudges.

5 Reposition the first stencil below or at the side of the last completed section, leaving space for the black of the second stencil to show around the edges. Continue to stencil the fabric until it is completely covered with pattern. To fill in small gaps use just the dots from the first stencil. Allow the paint to dry; refer to the manufacturer's recommended drying times. Clean the stencils with warm water after using them.

More ideas
You can use stencils to create other animal prints. The giraffe pattern featured below is made up of assorted, rounded-off, square shapes which gradually become smaller. Copy tiger and zebra stripes from children's books or magazines. Use these ideas to decorate furniture, trinket boxes and even walls.

Remnants of white linen may be painted to cover dining chairs. Outline the zebra pattern in pencil and paint it in by hand using a stiff artist's flat brush.

Black staggered stripes stenciled on to tan-colored washed cotton produce an unusual tiger throw for any room in the house.

This giraffe print is stenciled on to a background of caramel cotton velvet in rich chamois brown, to create a pair of luxurious cushions.

TIPS

If you find the idea of using two stencils daunting, use a deeper shade of fabric, like the mock suede in the bedspread, and only use the second stencil. Pearlized or metallic fabric paints complement the texture of the fabrics perfectly. Most fabric paints have to be fixed by heat, and they can then be washed or drycleaned (check the label). Simply place a clean cotton cloth over the completed stencil and heat-seal with a hot iron.

Sponged lamp base

CHECKLIST

- *ceramic lamp base*
- *fine-grade sandpaper*
- *enamel paint: peach, country blue*
- *sea sponge*
- *distilled turpentine*
- *gloss or satin acrylic spray varnish*

PREPARATION

Clean the lamp base thoroughly to remove any dirt or grease, which would prevent paint from adhering.

L amps can add warmth and ambience to a home, but finding a lamp base to match your decor is not always easy. However, don't despair! Why not decorate a plain-colored base? If you have a lamp which has lost its appeal or is now old fashioned, you can give it a stylish facelift. A sea sponge and some enamel paints are all you will need. In this project, fresh peach and country blue are used on a white ceramic base.

1 *Tear a sheet of fine-grade sandpaper in half and fold it over again. Rub this over the surface of the lamp base in a gentle circular motion. This will roughen up the surface slightly and give it a good key for the paint to adhere. Try not to scratch and damage the surface as this will show through the paint. Dust the base after sanding.*

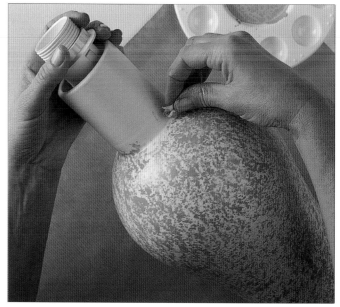

2 *Dampen the sea sponge and then dip it lightly in the peach enamel paint. Gently dab the sponge on to the lamp base, using a circular motion, leaving spaces between the pattern. Continue to re-apply the paint covering the entire base of the lamp.*

3 *If you have a sharp join at the neck, tear off a small piece of sea sponge and dip it into the peach paint. Carefully dab the paint around the seam. Then, using the original sponge, continue to apply the paint up to the edge of the lamp fitting.*

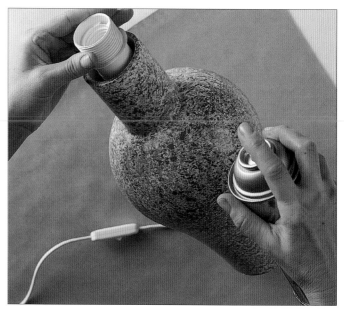

4 *Wash out the sponge with distilled turpentine. Rinse in water, squeezing out the excess. Sponge on the country blue enamel paint as before but apply less paint to the base so that you achieve an equal balance of the two colors.*

5 *Allow the base to dry. Then, holding the top of the lamp fitting in one hand, spray on an even coat of acrylic gloss or satin varnish. Turn the base around while spraying so it is entirely covered. Allow to dry.*

Oriental table

Oriental style is a popular influence in western design, creating an "east meets west" theme. Traditionally, rich reds and golds represent prosperity and good fortune, while the eastern symbols of birds and lotus flowers create attractive stylized patterns. The typical lacquered gloss finish has a very high sheen and is extremely hardwearing. Lacquer varnish is obtainable in both oil-based and quicker drying acrylic forms. Once you have decorated a table, you can go on to create an entire room of eastern magic; chairs, cupboards, head boards and even floors and walls can be decorated using this method.

1 Coat the paint roller evenly with red latex paint and apply over the entire table, starting with the underside and proceeding to the legs. Leave to dry, then rub fine sandpaper over the surface. Apply a second coat and allow to dry.

2 Using your thumb, smudge the black acrylic paint along the edges of the table and down the inside and outside curves of the legs. Gently pass a damp cloth over the smudged paint to blend it into the red. This will 'age' the table.

3 *Trace the template on page 77, then enlarge it to the required size using a photocopier. Position a piece of transfer paper, chalk-side down, on the corner of the table. Place the traced design on top, aligning the corners. Draw along all the lines of the design. Carefully peel back the transfer paper to reveal the blue outline of the pattern on the painted surface of the table.*

4 *Remove the tracing and transfer paper. Load a round artist's brush with the gold acrylic and paint along the outlined edges of the pattern first, then fill in the centers. Work from left to right, if you are right-handed, so that you do not smudge the wet paint. When dry, apply a second coat if necessary.*

5 *Once the paint is dry, outline the gold pattern in black. Using an artist's liner brush, dip the tip in water then load a small amount of black paint. Carefully pull a line around all the gold edges. Paint small teardrops inside the larger gold areas and feather shapes outside the drawn pattern. Allow to dry before wiping the table free of dust.*

6 *Load a varnish brush with lacquer varnish and start painting the table at the underside. Paint quickly and evenly in one direction. Do not overbrush. Allow to dry according to the manufacturer's instructions. Acrylic lacquer should be buffed to a sheen with a soft cloth. Oil-based lacquer will cure to a high sheen by itself if it is left to dry.*

Frosted glass panel

CHECKLIST

- *paint thinner*
- *glass panel, ¼ in (6mm) thick*
- *tracing paper*
- *cutting mat*
- *stencilling acetate*
- *permanent pen*
- *craft knife*
- *spray mount*
- *frosting varnish*
- *paint tray*
- *nylon decorator's brush*
- *mini roller with foam sleeve*
- *tweezers*

PREPARATION

Pour some paint thinner on to a cotton cloth folded into a pad. Use this to clean the glass. Leave to dry.

Beautiful Victorian etched windows can often be seen in old hotels and pubs showing dancing figures, flowers and intricate borders. This project shows how to reproduce the effect of etched glass using the simple method of frosting varnish. The technique is unusual but simple to master and the glass can easily be cleaned with warm soapy water. This design features luxurious lilies drawn in a 1930s style, to create the illusion of tranquil summer days.

1 *Trace the template on page 77 and enlarge it to the required size. You will need a 2in (5cm) space between the edge of the glass and the pattern. Place the photocopy on a cutting mat, then lay a piece of stencilling acetate on top. Trace around the outlines with a permanent pen. Cut along the pen lines using a craft knife. Reserve the cut-out pieces.*

Ensure that the glass is at room temperature and 2
completely dry. Working in a well-ventilated area and
wearing a protective face mask, spray the back of each
cut-out piece of the pattern with spray mount. Stick each
pattern piece to the glass, referring to the photocopy of
the design to achieve the correct placement.

3 Shake the bottle of frosting varnish and pour a small
amount of it into a paint tray. Using a nylon decorator's
brush, apply a thick, even coat of frosting varnish over the
entire surface of the glass. Allow the varnish to dry for a
few moments before proceeding to the next step.

4 Check that the foam sleeve is clean and dust free.
Gently run the dry roller over the varnished surface of
the glass; this will remove any brushmarks and even out
the coverage. This process will also produce the etched
textured appearance.

5 Before the varnish hardens, remove the pieces of acetate. This can be tricky as the latex in the varnish will start to stick to the acetate as it dries; you might find it easier to use tweezers to do this. Slide the craft knife blade under the edge of each piece and secure the other end of each piece with the tweezers. Slowly lift it away from the glass so that you avoid touching the varnish and spoiling the frosting effect. If some frosting should start to come away with the stencil, cut it with the craft knife and press it back down.

TIPS

If you desire a more densely etched area on your glass, apply a second coat of frosting varnish after allowing the first coat to dry. Roll the varnish as above.

More ideas
Many glass pieces in the home can be decorated with frosting varnish, including mirrors, windows and vases. Alternatively, be inspired by all the varieties of colorful paints, enamels and decorative sprays. Create a focal piece, like the tabletop or Gothic-style mirror with vibrant tangerine or parrot green.

This rich Gothic mirror is given a burnt orange wash over a terracotta background with a Gothic-style stencil painted on to the glass.

Transform a plain glass tabletop with enamel paints in bright vibrant colors like metallic blue, rose, tangerine and green. Turn over to protect the surface.

Revive an old bathroom cabinet with sea-theme stencils. Cover the surrounding area and spray glass with aquatic blue paint.

- *sandpaper*
- *corner cupboard*
- *latex paint: Terracotta (satin finish); off-white (flat or eggshell finish)*
- *artist acrylic paint: burnt umber, sap green, naples yellow, burnt sienna, black*
- *acrylic transparent glaze*
- *nylon decorator's brush*
- *graining tool*
- *paper*
- *manilla card stock*
- *spray mount/masking tape*
- *chalk*
- *round artist's brush, no.8*
- *furniture wax*

PREPARATION

Rub the cupboard down with sandpaper. Then paint inside and out with terracotta latex paint. When dry, paint the front door panel using the off-white latex and leave to dry. Apply a second coat if necessary. When dry, outline the off-white area with black acrylic paint.

Topiary cupboard

Topiary is the art of clipping trees and shrubs into shapes, and it has been practiced since the first century. The first real topiary revival took place in renaissance Italy, where the shapes created ranged from simple spheres to complicated human figures, urns, and birds. This corner cupboard is transformed by an attractive topiary design. Add the Latin name using a tracing-off technique.

1 *Mix a glaze for graining: 1 part burnt sienna acrylic and 3 parts acrylic transparent glaze. Apply the glaze over the cupboard using a nylon decorator's brush, and then feather out all brushstrokes. Press the graining tool at the top of the cupboard and sweep it down through the glaze using a rocking motion. A wood grain effect will appear. Repeat until you have covered the cupboard. Leave this to dry.*

2 On paper, draw around a cup and then move the cup about 1½in (4cm) to the right. Draw another circle and join to create the oval shape. Draw two more ovals above the first, decreasing in size, and join all with a single stem. Draw a plant pot. Trace the design on to card stock and cut out.

3 Use spray mount to secure the card to the door. Draw a thin chalk line around it and remove. Mix two shades of green using sap green and naples yellow. Paint the tree using a round artist's brush; paint the pot and tree branch with terracotta latex paint and shade with sienna artist's acrylic.

4 When the tree is dry, mix 2-3 drops of burnt umber acrylic with a teaspoon of glaze. Using your thumb, age the cupboard by smudging the glaze around the handle and edges where the door would have worn. Repeat around the left-hand side of the topiary shapes.

5 Rub fine sandpaper gently over the painted areas on the cupboard door to age the design by removing small areas of paint. Using a soft cotton cloth, apply clear furniture wax over the entire surface of the cupboard. Buff to a soft sheen.

Mexican painted pot

The magic of Mexico can be captured with vibrant colors: sunshine yellows, tomato reds and pepper greens. Remote Indian communities still paint walls and furniture in styles which date back to the ancient Aztec traditions. Terracotta pots are the perfect objects to paint as the Mexican designs are simple, colorful and very easy to reproduce. A cactus plant placed in the pot will complete the truly authentic Mexican feel.

CHECKLIST

- *terracotta pot*
- *PVA glue*
- *decorator's brush*
- *chalk*
- *artist acrylic paints: hooker's green, white, cadmium yellow, cadmium red, burnt orange, pthalo turquoise*
- *artist's brushes: flat, no.8; liner, no.1*
- *manilla card stock*
- *masking tape*
- *polyurethane spray varnish*

PREPARATION

Wipe the surface of the terracotta pot to ensure that it is clean and then leave to dry.

1 *Dilute PVA glue in the proportion of 1 part PVA to 5 parts water. Using a decorator's brush, paint this mixture liberally over the surface of the pot; this will make the surface less porous and provide a key for the paint to adhere. Leave to dry.*

2 Place a cup next to the pot and rest a piece of chalk on the top of the cup. Holding both, pull the chalk around the pot to draw a level chalk line. Repeat this process using a taller cup to create a chalked band for you to use as a guide for painting between.

3 Paint the marked band with a mixture of hooker's green and white acrylic paint using an artist's large flat brush. Apply in watery, sweeping strokes. When dry, paint V-shapes in cadmium yellow. These shapes do not have to be symmetrical. Outline each V with a fine line of cadmium red. Leave to dry.

4 To make a step pattern, enlarge the template (see page 77) to fit the circumference of your pot. To achieve a primitive look, make the lines slightly crooked as you cut the template from manilla card stock. Stick the template in place with masking tape and draw around both the inside and outside edges of the card with chalk.

5 Using the artist flat, mix burnt orange acrylic with white and paint one brush width around the outside of the chalk lines, and fill in the diamond shape in the center. Paint the space between with a mixture of white and turquoise acrylic. When dry, paint a cross in the middle diamond in an alternative color. Protect with matte varnish.

TEMPLATES

TO USE THESE TEMPLATES, ENLARGE THEM AS NECESSARY USING A PHOTOCOPIER,
THEN TRACE OFF AND USE AS SPECIFIED IN THE PROJECTS.

LEOPARD STENCIL 1

LEOPARD STENCIL 2

GLOSSARY

ACRYLIC GOLD SIZE: *This medium is used for applying metal or gold transfer leaf. It is easier to use and dries more quickly than the traditional oil-based equivalent.*

ACRYLIC VARNISH: *Acrylic varnish is available with a flat, satin or gloss finish. When applied, it looks milky, but it becomes transparent when dry. Acrylic varnish does not turn yellow like oil-based varnish but remains durable and heat resistant.*

ACRYLIC VARNISH BRUSHES: *These are made from nylon and are very fine. They do not leave brushstrokes.*

AGEING: *This is a term used to describe the techniques for making a newly painted piece look older than it is.*

ARTIST'S ACRYLIC PAINT: *This paint is available in tubes at good art shops. It is quick to dry and is good for painting and stencilling.*

ARTIST'S BRUSHES: *Available in different sizes, artist's brushes are ideal for painting details. Made from squirrel hair, the bristles do not separate.*

CALLIGRAPHY BRUSHES: *These are specially designed for the art of calligraphy; each brush can paint wide or narrow strokes. The traditional brush is made from bamboo, with a casing to protect the delicate hair tip.*

CALLIGRAPHY INK: *This is a stable ink which is available in a range of colors. Some black inks bleed when acrylic varnish is applied; use a spray varnish to seal these.*

CENTER PUNCH: *This is used for marking holes on sheet metal and is available from hardware stores.*

CERAMIC PAINT: *This paint is especially made for painting on ceramics and is available in liquid or spray form. The paint can be cleaned off using distilled turpentine or paint thinner.*

COLORIZERS: *These come in small tubes and can be mixed with latex and acrylic mediums. They are very strong and effective, with unusual pearlized and metallic finishes.*

CONTOUR OUTLINING MEDIUM: *Available in tubes of grey, silver or gold, this medium makes a built-up outline for glass paint. It can be cleaned off using distilled turpentine.*

CRACKLE GLAZE: *This is a transparent acrylic medium, which is brushed between two coats of paint, causing the second coat of paint to separate and crack, thus exposing the base coat. This medium should not be confused with craquelure or crackle varnish.*

DÉCOUPAGE: *This is an old Victorian technique which literally means "to cut out", and it involves decorating a surface using cut-out paper images. The Victorians built up the finished surface with many coats of varnish, until there was no variation in the surface texture, to create a hand-painted look.*

ENAMEL PAINT: *This is a hard-wearing paint which dries to a glossy finish.*

FABRIC PAINT: *This paint is formulated for painting on fabric. Most fabric paints need to be fixed by heat, either by ironing or steaming; refer to the specific manufacturer's instructions.*

FROSTING VARNISH: *A latex medium which dries to an etched frosty look.*

GESSO: *Gesso is a mixture of whiting and glue and can be bought ready-made in art shops and some decorating stores. It provides a glass-smooth surface to paint on and, once applied, dries very quickly.*

GILDING: *This is the technique of applying gold leaf and metal transfer leaf to almost any surface. Transfer leaf is easy to manage for beginners. Gold leaf comes in books of approximately 25 sheets; the leaf is on separate squares of delicate tissue paper.*

GILDING BRUSHES: *An artisan flat number 10 is a good alternative to a gilding brush for applying the transfer gold leaf.*

GLASS PAINT: *This is available in a variety of colors and effects. Use it in conjunction with contour outlining medium for painting stained-glass effects on glassware.*

GRAINING TOOL: *A tool used to create effects of wood grain in wet glaze. The raised areas create softwood patterns.*

LACQUER: *Available in acrylic or oil-based forms, lacquer varnish dries to a highly polished finish.*

LATEX PAINT: *This is a versatile water-based household paint which can be used on most surfaces. Flat latex paint adheres best because of its consistency, and it can be rubbed back easily to provide a smooth finish. It must be sealed when the item is finished.*

PVA GLUE: *A white water based glue that dries clear and gives a strong bond.*

SHEET METAL: *Available from hardware stores, sheet metal has an attractive smooth finish, is easy to cut with tin snips, and can be polished to a shine when finished. It is ideal for creating punched tin effects.*

SOFTENING BRUSH: *A soft-bristled brush with a wide flat head, used for softening and feathering the edges of a faux finish.*

SPRAY MOUNT: *This is a glue which is sprayed rather than brushed on to a surface. It is useful for spraying on to the underside of a stencil to secure it while stencilling.*

SPRAY PAINT: *Some decorative spray paints are non-toxic and suitable for children's toys and furniture. They are available in a wide range of colors and they dry quickly. Spray painting is best carried out outside or in a well-ventilated room, making sure that all surrounding areas are covered.*

SPRAY VARNISH: *Available in flat, satin and gloss finish, spray varnish is easy to apply and dries quickly. It is useful for spraying on pictures or photocopies to prevent ink bleeding. Spray varnish is unsuitable on white paints as it can yellow with age.*

STAMPING: *This is a technique of printing using a rubber or wooden stamp. Stamp companies manufacture a wide variety of ready-made stamps and most companies will make stamps following your design or pattern.*

STENCIL BRUSHES: *These stumpy-shaped brushes are obtainable in varying sizes. The bristles are designed for stippling or "rubbing" paint through a cut stencil.*

STENCIL FABRIC PAINT: *Used for hand-painting or stencilling on to fabric, stencil fabric paint is washable and easy to apply using a swirling motion. Read the manufacturer's instructions on fixing.*

STENCILLING: *Stencilling is the technique of decorating a surface using paint and a cut stencil. Stencils are readily available or you can make your own using template plastic or manilla card stock.*

STENCIL PAINT: *Water-based stencil paints come in small plastic bottles and come in a wide range of colors. Tubes of artist's acrylic paints can also be used. Oil-based stencil sticks are easy to use and are good for blending and shading but this paint takes longer to dry.*

TEMPLATE PLASTIC/CARD: *Template plastic is sold by the sheet or on a roll; it is transparent and easy to work with. Manilla card stock can also be used as an alternative. Both are obtainable from art shops.*

TIN SNIPS: *Used for cutting sheet metal, they are available from hardware stores..*

TRACING PAPER: *Essential for transferring designs, tracing stencils, calligraphy and making templates.*

TRANSFER PAPER: *This has a chalky blue film on one side. To use it, place the paper film side down, lay your pattern on top, and draw over the outlines with a sharp pencil. The lines will be transferred to the surface underneath.*

VARNISHING WAX: *This thin milky liquid is painted on to an object to seal it. When dry, it gives the appearance of an old waxed finish. It can be polished to a high shine.*

WAX: *Good quality furniture waxes are ideal for sealing painted surfaces and giving a smooth finish. The most common waxes used are clear and neutral. Clear wax leaves a creamy finish; neutral is ideal for liming and pale blues. Ageing waxes are available in darker shades.*

S U P P L I E R S

2000 Art Supplies
www.2000-art.com
*Extensive selection of
acrylic, oil, watercolor, and
ceramic paints,
canvas, brushes and more.
On-line catalog.*

All Seasons Company
www.allseasons.com
888 Brannan #1160
San Francisco, CA 94103
Tel. 415-864-3308
Fax. 415-864-5001
*Beads, sequins, rhinestones,
diamantes, jeweler's wire,
adhesives, findings.*

Artglass
www.artglass-source.com
Tel. 518-371-0977
Fax. 518-371-9423
*Tiles, grout, cutters, adhesives
and supplies for mosaic work.*

Ben Franklin Crafts
www.benfranklinstores.com
*Nationwide chain of crafts
stores; extensive selection of
stenciling, decoupage,
gilding, stamping and
painting supplies. Web site
provides directory of stores.*

**Crafter's Components
Catalog**
www.lamp-specialties.com
Tel. 800-CALL-LAMP
*Complete resources for crafters
including ceramic work, frame
blanks, paints, beads, mosaics,
brushes and more.*

Dover Publications
31 East 2nd Street
Mineola, NY 11501
Tel. 516-294-7000
Fax. 516-742-5049
*Extensive selection of art books
containing copyright-free
lithographs, typography sets,
frames, borders and other
images for decoupage, transfer
and other design work.*

**Effie Glitzfinger's
St. Louis Stamp Design**
www.glitzfinger.com
12906 Barbezieus Drive
St. Louis, MO 63141
Tel. 800-450-8586
Fax. 800-450-0185
*Templates, brushes, paints,
suplies for stenciling
projects.*

Fascinating Folds
www.fascinating-folds.com
P.O. Box 10070
Glendale, AZ 85318
Tel. 800-968-2418
*Supplies for decoupage,
quilling, parchment and
other paper craft, including
embossing metals, florist
foils, reproduction
documents, vintage nautical
maps and more.*

Faux Like A Pro
www.fauxlikeapro.com
Tel. 617-713-4320
*Complete line of paints, glazes,
brushes, tools and accessories
for faux-finish painting.*

Lee Valley & Veritas
www.leevalley.com
Fine woodworking and
Gardening Tools
P.O. Box 1780
Ogdensburg, NY 13669
Tel. 800-871-8158
Fax. 800-513-7885
*Fine woodworking tools,
fittings, and supplies, garden
supplies and furnishings.*

Liming Wax
Briwax
www.briwaxwoodcave.com
1-800-BRIWAX-X

Mylands Wax
www.mylands.com
1-888-3MYLAND

Mosaic Mercantile
www.mosaicmerc.com
*Wholesale supplier of tiles,
grout, ceramic paint, and
tools. $250 minimum order.
On-line search engine lists
retail outlets.*

Mylands Wax
www.mylands.com
1-888-3MYLAND
P.O. Box 1166
Collierville, TN 38027-1166
Liming wax

Nancy's Notions
www.nancysnotions.com
333 Beichl Avenue
P.O. Box 683
Beaver Dam WI 53916
*Fusible web, quilter's tape,
sewing accessories and
notions for sewing.*

Staedtler, Inc.
21900 Plummer Street
Chatsworth, CA 91311
Tel. 800-800-3691
Fax. 800-675-8249
*Watercolor pan sets, brushes,
markers, calligraphy pens.*

Stencil-Ease
www.stencilease.com
P.O. Box 1127
Old Saybrook, CT 06475
Tel. 860-395-0150
Fax. 860-395-0166
*Complete assortment of
brushes, stencils, templates,
paints and stenciling supplies.*

**Woodtown Unfinished
Furniture**
www.woodtownusa.com
13951 Riverview Drive
Elk River, MN 55330
Tel./Fax 800-510-WOOD
*On-line catalog of unfinished
furniture and accessories.*

Uhlfelder Gold Leaf
www.uhlfeldergoldleaf.com
420 South Fulton Avenue
Mount Vernon, NY 10553
Tel. 800-664-LUCO
Fax. 914-664-8721
*High quality gold leaf and
other gilding and art supplies.*

USArtQuest, Inc.
www.usartquest.com
Tel. 800-200-7848
Fax. 517-522-6225
*Art brushes, paints, canvas,
art paper, supplies.*

INDEX

A

acrylic paint:
antiqued key box, 9
children's chair, 16-19
chrome-effect frames, 52
classic tray, 10-12
Eastern treasure chest, 34
marbled plaster pieces, 48
Mexican painted pot, 74
Oriental table, 63-4
topiary cupboard, 70-2
voile curtain, 54
ageing effect, 63
animal prints, 56-9
antiqued key box, 6-9

B

bronzing, 29

C

calligraphy, 36-9
ceramic paint, 30-2
children's chair, 16-9
chrome-effect frames, 50-2
chrome-effect paint, 29, 50
classic tray, 10-12
crackle medium, 8, 9
curtains, easy fabric, 24

D

découpage, 8-9, 10-12
distressing, paint effect, 34

E

emulsion paint:
antiqued key box, 6-9
Eastern treasure chest, 33-4
jewelry box, 38-9
marbled plaster pieces, 46
Oriental table, 63
tin-panelled cupboard, 43-4
topiary cupboard, 70-2
verdigris candlestick, 26-9
etched glass effect, 66-9

F

frosted glass panel, 66-9

G

gesso, 36
gilded curtain pole, 23-5
glass painting, 13-14
glues:
epoxy resin, 44
glitter, 54
PVA, 73
gold leaf and size, 24
graining, 70
grapes and vines water set, 13-15

I

Indian temple cushions, 40-2

J

jewelry box, 36-9

L

lacquer, 49, 63, 64
limed picture frame, 20-2

M

marbled plaster pieces, 46-9
Mexican painted pot, 73-5

O

Oriental table, 63-5

P

paints:
acrylic see acrylic paint
ceramic, 30-2
emulsion see emulsion paint
enamel, 30, 50-2, 62
fabric, 42, 58-9
metallic, 19, 29, 42, 54
red oxide, 23
photocopies, 8-9, 10-12, 66

S

scumble glaze, 48, 70
sheet metal, 43-4
silk painting, 40-2
size, acrylic gold, 24
sponged lamp base, 60-2
stained glass window effects, 14
stamped ceramic tiles, 30-2
stamping and stamps, 19, 30-2
stencil sticks, 28
stenciled animal prints, 56-9
stenciling, 16-19, 40-2, 56-9, 66-9

T

tin-panelled cupboard, 43-5
topiary cupboard, 70-2
transfer paper, 38, 64
treasure chest, 33-4

V

varnish: acrylic
antiqued key box, 8, 9
children's chair, 19
classic tray, 10-12
gilded curtain pole, 24
jewelry box, 39
marbled plaster pieces, 49
Mexican painted pot, 74
sponged lamp base, 62
verdigris candlestick, 29
frosting, 66-9
lacquer, 63, 64
polyurethane, 74
verdigris candlestick, 26-9
voile curtain, 53-5

W

wax:
acrylic/furniture, 9, 22, 34, 72
gilt, 28
wood grain:
effect, 70
opening up, 20